CORNERSTONES OF FREEDOM™

BILL CLINTON

BY JOSH GREGORY

CHILDREN'S PRESS®
An Imprint of Scholastic Inc.
New York Toronto London Auckland Sydney
Mexico City New Delhi Hong Kong
Danbury, Connecticut

BRINGING HISTORY to LIFE

Content Consultant
James Marten, PhD
Professor and Chair, History Department
Marquette University
Milwaukee, Wisconsin

Library of Congress Cataloging-in-Publication Data
Gregory, Josh.
Bill Clinton / By Josh Gregory.
pages cm. — (Cornerstones of freedom)
Includes bibliographical references and index.
ISBN 978-0-531-21329-2 (lib. bdg.) — ISBN 978-0-531-25825-5 (pbk.)
1. Clinton, Bill, 1946– —Juvenile literature. 2. Presidents—United States—
Biography—Juvenile literature. I. Title.
E886.G755 2014
973.929092—dc23[B]   2013019581

SCHOLASTIC, CHILDREN'S PRESS, CORNERSTONES OF FREEDOM™,
and associated logos are trademarks and/or registered trademarks of
Scholastic Inc.

 2 3 4 5 6 7 8 9 10 R 23 22 21 20 19 18 17 16 15 14

Photographs ©: Alamy Images: 20 (James Osmond), 4 bottom, 44
(Richard Ellis); AP Images: 30 (Bob Galbraith), 46 (Charles Rex Arbogast),
28, 31 (Danny Johnston), 15 (Henry Griffin), 18 (ho), 40, 48 (Joe Marquette),
5 bottom, 11 (Mike Stewart), 6 (Rex Features), 34 (Ric Feld), 35 (Richard
Drew), 47 (Ron Edmonds), 2 – 3, 32 (Stephan Savoia); Corbis Images/
Mike Stewart/Sygma: 4 top, 23, 27; Georgetown University Archives:
9; Getty Images: 16 (Arnold Sachs), 38 (J. David Ake/AFP), 24, 57 top
(Mandel Ngan/AFP), 37, 57 bottom (Peter Kramer/NBC), 54 (Richard Ellis/
AFP), 7 (Saul Loeb/AFP), 51 (Thony Belizaire/AFP), 36 (Tim Clary/AFP),
55 (Win McNamee for The Clinton Foundation); National Archives and
Records Administration: 5, 8, 10, 12, 13, 14, 22, 26, 41, 43, 56 (Courtesy
William J. Clinton Presidential Library), 25 (University of Arkansas Special
Collections); Newscom/Jim Macmillan/KRT: 39; Reuters: back cover
(Blake Sell), cover (Kevin Lamarque).

Maps by XNR Productions, Inc.

Did you know that studying history can be fun?

BRING HISTORY TO LIFE by becoming a history investigator. Examine the evidence (primary and secondary source materials); cross-examine the people and witnesses. Take a look at what was happening at the time—but be careful! What happened years ago might suddenly become incredibly interesting and change the way you think!

Contents

Not Forgotten

Former president Bill Clinton received enthusiastic applause as he took the stage at the 2012 Democratic National Convention.

On the evening of September 5, 2012, former U.S. president Bill Clinton took the stage at the Democratic National Convention. This meeting is held every four years to officially determine the Democratic Party's candidate in the next presidential election. Clinton was there to speak in support of the party's candidate that year, **incumbent** president Barack Obama. Obama faced a difficult election against Republican challenger Mitt Romney.

Though it had been nearly 12 years since Clinton had completed his second term, his opinion still meant a great deal to the American people. The crowd at the convention and television viewers at home listened carefully as Clinton spoke for almost an hour about some of the most important political issues of the day. Though many of the topics he discussed were complicated, he used facts to outline his message in a simple, direct way that appealed to voters of many different backgrounds and political beliefs. The crowd erupted in applause as Clinton finished his speech and embraced President Obama. Across the nation, Americans were reminded why they had chosen Clinton as the nation's 42nd president all those years before.

Bill Clinton's support helped contribute to President Barack Obama's reelection.

CONVENTION WAS HELD IN CHARLOTTE, N.C.

CHAPTER I

A HOPEFUL BEGINNING

Bill Clinton was born to a widowed single mother.

BILL CLINTON WAS BORN

William Jefferson Blythe III on August 19, 1946, in Hope, Arkansas. Hope was a small town with a population of around 8,000 people. Virginia Cassidy Blythe was pregnant with Bill when his father, William Jefferson Blythe, was killed in an automobile accident. As a result, young Bill never got the chance to meet his biological father. This would have a lasting impact on the future president. "My father left me with the feeling that I had to live for two people," he later wrote, "and that if I did it well enough, somehow I could make up for the life he should have had."

As a child, Bill Clinton was called Billy by his friends and relatives.

Lessons Learned

Virginia brought her newborn son home, where she lived with her parents, Eldridge and Edith Cassidy. She knew that she would need a good job to earn enough money to move into her own home and provide for Bill. Before Bill was born, she had worked as a nurse, so she decided to expand her skills. This would allow her to earn more money as a nurse. When Bill was about two years old, she moved to New Orleans, Louisiana, to attend nursing school. Bill stayed behind with his grandparents.

Eldridge and Edith were strict, but they loved Bill very much. Clinton later wrote, "My grandparents and my mother always made me feel I was the most important person in the world to them." The Cassidys believed strongly in the importance of a good education. They helped Bill learn to read when he was only three years old.

The Cassidys also taught their grandson valuable life lessons that would come to have a major effect on his political beliefs. They owned a small grocery store just outside of Hope, where they often allowed customers who were low on money to purchase groceries on credit. This means that those customers could take the groceries when they needed them and pay for them later. Virginia later remembered Eldridge telling her that "good people who were doing the best they could deserved to be able to feed their families."

William Jefferson Blythe

William Jefferson Blythe met Virginia Cassidy in 1943, when he brought a friend to the hospital where Virginia was training to be a nurse. They were married two months later, but Blythe had to leave for Europe almost immediately to serve in World War II (1939–1945).

When Blythe returned from the war in 1945, he and Virginia moved to Chicago, Illinois. They soon purchased a home but could not move in right away. Because she was pregnant, Virginia decided to return to Arkansas until the house was ready. On May 17, 1946, Blythe was on his way to Arkansas to pick her up to move into their new home. His tire blew out while driving on a wet road at night. He died in the resulting crash.

Bill's half brother, Roger Clinton Jr., was born in 1956.

This lesson had an impact on young Bill, who spent much of his life working to help people in need.

A Changing Family

Virginia finished school and returned to Arkansas in 1950. She was ready to begin her career as a nurse anesthetist. Later that year, she married a man named Roger Clinton. Roger was the owner of a local car dealership. Virginia, Roger, and Bill became a family. In 1952, they moved to Hot Springs, Arkansas, about 80 miles (130 kilometers) away from Hope.

Driven by his grandparents' focus on education, Bill was a good student at school. He also started going to church at a young age, even though no one else in his family was religious. Every Sunday, he walked half a mile (1 km) by himself to attend church services. There, he developed a love of music. The gospel songs Bill heard at church inspired him to take lessons on the saxophone, an instrument he continued to play throughout his life.

School Days

Bill began high school in 1960. As usual, he was an excellent student. He was popular among his fellow students and participated in many school activities. Music was one of his greatest passions. His saxophone skills made him a star in the school's jazz band. He also played in the marching band and concert band. He loved all kinds of music, from classical to jazz to rock and roll.

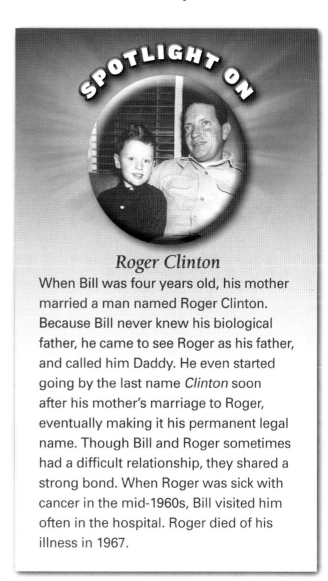

SPOTLIGHT ON

Roger Clinton

When Bill was four years old, his mother married a man named Roger Clinton. Because Bill never knew his biological father, he came to see Roger as his father, and called him Daddy. He even started going by the last name *Clinton* soon after his mother's marriage to Roger, eventually making it his permanent legal name. Though Bill and Roger sometimes had a difficult relationship, they shared a strong bond. When Roger was sick with cancer in the mid-1960s, Bill visited him often in the hospital. Roger died of his illness in 1967.

Bill also participated in his school government. He had long been fascinated by politics. By the time he was 10, he was watching speeches and debates on television. Bill's political interest grew during high school. In his junior year, he was voted class president.

In 1963, Bill was chosen by his teachers to participate in Arkansas Boys State. This was a yearly camp where the state's top students gathered to learn about government. As part of the program, the camp held elections to

When he was a boy, Bill Clinton hoped to one day become a professional musician.

J. William Fulbright was one of Bill Clinton's first political mentors.

choose representatives. Those chosen would attend a national meeting of boys from each of the other states' camps. Bill won the election, giving him the chance to travel to Washington, D.C., for the meeting.

In Washington, D.C., Bill debated the major political issues of the time with boys from other states and toured some of the nation's most famous landmarks. He also got to meet with Arkansas's senators. One of them was J. William Fulbright, who held an important position as chairman of the Senate Foreign Relations Committee.

One of the most exciting events of the trip came on July 24, when the group of boys visited the White House to meet President John F. Kennedy. Fearing that

Getting to meet President John F. Kennedy was a thrilling moment for young Bill Clinton.

the president might not have time to greet the boys individually, Bill made sure he was at the front of the pack when the president arrived. This gave the young future president an opportunity to shake hands with Kennedy, who was one of his greatest heroes. "It was an amazing moment for me," he later wrote.

A month after returning home from Washington, D.C., Bill witnessed another event that would encourage him to become a politician. On August 28, 1963, Dr. Martin Luther King Jr. delivered his famous "I Have a Dream" speech from the steps of the Lincoln Memorial in Washington, D.C. The speech dealt with the civil rights movement, which sought to secure equal treatment for African Americans. Bill watched the speech from home on television. He was so moved and impressed by it that he memorized the whole speech.

College and Beyond

In 1964, Bill returned to Washington, D.C., to begin college at Georgetown University. There, he studied international affairs and became an active participant in student politics. This led to his election as president of both his freshman and sophomore classes.

At the end of his sophomore year, Bill returned home to Arkansas, where he hoped to participate in a larger political campaign. He got a job working for the campaign of Frank Holt, a Democrat who was running

A FIRSTHAND LOOK AT
MARTIN LUTHER KING JR.'S "I HAVE A DREAM" SPEECH

Martin Luther King Jr.'s "I Have a Dream" speech was one of the most important events of the civil rights movement. Millions of people watched it at home on television, and it brought widespread attention to the importance of the movement. See page 60 for a link to read the full text of the speech online.

for governor. At first, Bill's job consisted mainly of simple tasks such as hanging up signs and handing out bumper stickers. He soon proved himself to be far too valuable for such a basic job.

At one campaign event, Holt was nowhere to be seen as his scheduled time to speak grew near. Bill tracked him down on the telephone and asked where he was. Holt explained that he had gotten held up and would not be able to make it to the event in time to deliver his speech. He asked Bill to speak in his place. Bill was nervous, but he did a good job explaining Holt's political goals and opinions to the audience. Holt was so impressed that he began asking Bill to speak at

Bill Clinton (left) poses with his fellow Georgetown student government leaders, secretary Andy Poole (center) and vice president Terry Modglin (right).

Bill Clinton returned to Georgetown University to deliver the commencement address in 1980.

other events. Holt eventually lost the election, but the campaign provided Bill with valuable experience.

Partially based on this experience, Bill secured a job as an intern for the Senate Foreign Relations Committee during his junior year at Georgetown. There, he worked under Senator J. William Fulbright, whom he had met during his Boys State trip in high school. Bill admired Fulbright and shared many of his political views. Fulbright was an important mentor as Bill learned about national politics from the inside. Bill continued working for the committee until he graduated from Georgetown in 1968. With a degree in hand, he could begin pursuing even bigger goals.

CHAPTER 2

THE LONG ROAD TO WASHINGTON, D.C.

The University of Oxford in England is one of the oldest universities in the world.

DURING CLINTON'S TIME AT Georgetown, he had proven himself to be one of the school's top students. His impressive academic performance earned him a Rhodes Scholarship. This highly prestigious award is given to only a few students each year. It provides them with the opportunity to study at the University of Oxford in Oxford, England, for two years. Clinton was thrilled to have such an opportunity. A few months after graduating from Georgetown, he moved to Oxford to begin his studies. For the next two years, he took courses to increase his knowledge of government.

Bill Clinton and Hillary Rodham met when they were both students at Yale Law School in Connecticut.

Love at Law School

Clinton returned home in 1970 and prepared for the next step of his education. That fall, he moved to New Haven, Connecticut, to study at Yale Law School, one of the most respected law schools in the United States.

One day, while he was sitting in the back of a class on civil rights, Clinton noticed a fellow student he had never seen before. He was impressed with her beauty and confidence. After class, he wanted to talk to her but found himself too nervous to get her attention. Over the next few days, he saw the young woman again and again in classes and at other campus activities, but he still couldn't work up the nerve to introduce himself.

Then, while Clinton was in the school library talking to another student, he noticed the woman standing across the room looking at a book. He stopped paying attention to his conversation because he could not stop looking at the woman. Eventually, she noticed that he was looking at her. She walked across the room and introduced herself. Clinton later remembered her telling him, "If you're going to keep staring at me and I'm going to keep staring back, we ought to at least know each other's names. Mine's Hillary Rodham." The two started dating soon after. Like Bill, Hillary was extremely interested in politics and hoped to run for office one day.

In addition to his law studies, Clinton continued to participate in politics at Yale. In 1972, he and Hillary

Bill Clinton and Hillary Rodham bonded over their shared political ambitions.

Hillary Rodham Clinton

Hillary Rodham was born in Chicago, Illinois, on October 26, 1947. She became interested in politics at a young age and supported the Republican Party during her high school years. Soon after starting college, however, she began to realize that her views were more closely aligned with the Democratic Party. By 1968, she had officially switched parties and began participating in the campaign of Democratic presidential candidate Eugene McCarthy.

After marrying Bill Clinton in 1975, Hillary continued to work on her own political causes while supporting her husband's career. Once Bill completed his second term as president in 2001, Hillary ran for U.S. Congress. She won the election and served two terms in the Senate before running for president in 2008. She was defeated in the Democratic **primary** elections by Barack Obama. However, Obama chose her to be the U.S. secretary of state. She served in that position until resigning in 2012.

both helped with the campaign of Democratic presidential candidate George McGovern. McGovern was running against the Republican incumbent Richard Nixon. Bill and Hillary headed to Texas, where they helped spread word of McGovern's campaign promises to end the Vietnam War (1954–1975) and increase opportunities for the nation's poor. In the end, McGovern lost the election to Nixon. However, Bill and Hillary learned a great deal about how to gather support for a candidate in a major national election.

1. INDIV OWNERSHIP
2. COMPETITION
3. PROFIT
4. PRODUCTION FOR MARKET ECONOMY

Bill Clinton taught college courses as he prepared to launch his political career.

Running for Office

Bill and Hillary graduated from Yale Law School in 1973. After graduation, Hillary took a job in Massachusetts while Bill began teaching at the University of Arkansas Law School in Fayetteville, Arkansas. Though they lived far apart, they stayed in touch as they pursued their individual goals.

As Clinton taught classes, he began setting his sights on political office. In 1974, he decided to run for one of Arkansas's seats in the U.S. House of Representatives. Hillary moved to Arkansas and got a job teaching at the same school as Bill to help him with his campaign.

Clinton lost the election, but it was a closer race than many people had anticipated. He didn't let the loss get him down. He was still very young, and he had plenty of time to run again in later elections. In addition, he knew that he had made valuable allies among some of the state's most powerful Democrats during the campaign.

Governor Clinton

Bill and Hillary decided to get married in 1975. On October 11, they held a small wedding ceremony in the living room of their home in Fayetteville.

The following year, Clinton decided to run for office once again. He had considered running for Congress

Bill Clinton was 29 years old when he married Hillary Rodham in 1975.

Hillary was an important part of Bill's campaign team when he ran for governor of Arkansas in 1978.

again but decided that he would rather stay in Arkansas, where he had many political allies. He ran for the office of Arkansas attorney general, the state's chief attorney and legal adviser. This time, he managed to win the election easily. In order for Bill to begin his new job, the Clintons moved to Little Rock, the state capital. There, Hillary got a job working at a law firm.

After his first term as attorney general, Clinton's political career was on the upswing. He decided to run for governor in 1978. After a successful campaign, he defeated Republican Lynn Lowe in the election. At 32 years old, Clinton was the youngest governor in the country and among the youngest the nation had ever seen.

In November 1982, Bill Clinton defeated Frank White to reclaim his position as governor of Arkansas.

During his first term, Clinton pursued many of the same political causes he had felt strongly about since he was a child. He hoped to improve the state's education and health care programs. However, the country was in a **recession** at the time. This made it difficult for Clinton to find enough money in the state's budget to pay for the improvements he wanted.

In addition, he also made several political mistakes during his first term. For example, to fund improvements to the state's roads, he raised tax rates on gasoline and increased the fees required to register vehicles. Already suffering financially from the recession, the state's voters were unhappy with these decisions.

In the midst of all this, the Clintons experienced one of the happiest moments of their lives when their daughter, Chelsea, was born on February 27, 1980. Unfortunately, the Clintons met with disappointment just a few months later, as Arkansas voters chose not to reelect Clinton as governor.

Back in Office

After finishing his term as governor, Clinton worked at a law firm. He enjoyed having a normal work schedule and more time to spend with his family, but he had his mind set on returning to the governor's seat. Not long after leaving office, he began working to earn back the trust of the voters he had disappointed. He traveled all around the state, delivering speeches. By the 1982 elections, the people of Arkansas were ready to trust him again. Clinton won the election and became governor once more.

This time, he knew what to expect once he was in office. He was much more effective at accomplishing his goals. Once again, he worked to improve education in the state. He raised teacher salaries, created a testing system to ensure that all of the state's schools met certain standards, and improved access to education for poor families.

Clinton also worked to improve Arkansas's **economy**. By offering tax breaks, or freedom from paying certain taxes, he encouraged companies to do business in the state. This provided job opportunities for the people of Arkansas.

YESTERDAY'S HEADLINES

Bill Clinton's national reputation grew with his popularity in Arkansas. He was invited to deliver the official nomination speech for presidential candidate Michael Dukakis at the 1988 Democratic National Convention. With people across the country watching, he unleashed a long, rambling speech that ended up boring most of the audience. The speech made him a joke across the country. Never one to give up easily, Clinton bounced back by appearing on *The Tonight Show Starring Johnny Carson* (above). On live television, Clinton joked about the speech and played his saxophone. The country was charmed by his sense of humor and easygoing attitude. With that, Clinton solidified his place as a major contender for the next presidential election.

Clinton's popularity continued to grow during his time as governor. He was reelected in 1984 and 1986. After that, Arkansas increased the length of the governor's term of office to four years. Clinton ran again in 1990, and he enjoyed yet another victory.

Clinton's success began drawing attention from around the country. By 1988, he was widely considered to be a serious candidate for the Democratic presidential nomination. However, he decided not to run for president that year. He knew that a presidential campaign would require him to work long hours away

In 1988, Bill Clinton decided to delay his presidential run so he could spend more time with his family.

from his family. He wanted to wait until Chelsea was older before he undertook such a commitment. Just a couple of years later, however, Clinton started to think that the time was right to launch the campaign of a lifetime.

A FIRSTHAND LOOK AT
BILL CLINTON'S 1988 DEMOCRATIC NATIONAL CONVENTION SPEECH

At the 1988 Democratic National Convention, Bill Clinton delivered what is considered one of the worst speeches of his career. Because of his normally strong speaking skills, it stands out as a rare blunder. See page 60 for a link to watch the speech online.

CHAPTER 3

COMEBACK KID

After more than a decade in office as governor of Arkansas, Bill Clinton decided to take the next step in his political career.

BY LATE 1991, BILL CLINTON knew that he was ready to begin a campaign for president in the 1992 election. After serving for more than a decade as the governor of Arkansas, he believed that he had enough experience to take on the bigger responsibility of leading the country. Clinton also disagreed with the policies of then president George H. W. Bush. He believed that his own ideas would improve the nation.

Scandal!

Clinton was the immediate front-runner in the Democratic primary elections. After all he had done for Arkansas's economy, Americans hoped that he could work the same magic on the rest of the country. In addition, when giving speeches and answering interview questions, he came across as friendly and as someone people could relate to. Clinton's powerful campaign organization and the support he got from some of the country's top Democrats also gave him an advantage over other candidates in the primaries.

This early lead was soon put to the test. In late January 1992, an Arkansas state employee named Gennifer Flowers claimed that she and Clinton had been romantically involved during Clinton's time as governor.

Clinton's persuasive speeches helped make him the front-runner in the 1992 Democratic primaries.

Gennifer Flowers's accusations caused a controversy that almost ruined Bill Clinton's 1992 presidential campaign.

The nation was shocked by this revelation, and Clinton's reputation was damaged.

Not long afterward, the press uncovered another harmful story from Clinton's past. During his first year at Oxford, he became eligible to be **drafted** into service in the Vietnam War. Clinton, who strongly opposed the war and had organized protests against it, avoided being drafted. When this news was made public in 1992, many voters were disappointed in Clinton. They believed that his actions showed a lack of willingness to defend his country.

Hillary Clinton helped her husband recover from the Gennifer Flowers scandal by sticking by his side through the embarrassing accusations.

Though these scandals were setbacks, they did not end Clinton's campaign. Bill and Hillary Clinton appeared together on national television to defend him against the accusations. They admitted that there had been difficulties in their marriage, but Hillary supported her husband. Bill pointed out that voters should pay more attention to his political achievements than to his personal life. Thanks in part to these arguments, popular opinion of Clinton began to improve. By the end of spring, it was clear that he would win the Democratic primary. Because he handled these scandals skillfully and regained his political popularity, Clinton called himself the Comeback Kid.

The General Election

That July, at the 1992 Democratic National Convention in New York, Clinton was chosen as the Democratic candidate for president. He selected Senator Al Gore of Tennessee to run as his vice president.

Clinton's main competition in the general election was Republican incumbent George H. W. Bush. A third candidate, Texas businessman Ross Perot, was also a major contender. He was running as an independent, not associated with any political party. Perot's participation was one of the Clinton campaign's biggest obstacles. **Polls** showed that voters strongly preferred Clinton to Bush overall. This was due in part to economic

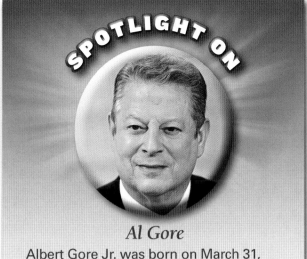

SPOTLIGHT ON

Al Gore

Albert Gore Jr. was born on March 31, 1948, in Washington, D.C. His father, Albert Gore Sr., was a U.S. senator from Tennessee. After attending college and serving in the Vietnam War, the younger Gore followed in his father's footsteps and ran for a seat in Congress. He served in the House of Representatives from 1977 until 1985. He was a member of the Senate from 1985 until 1993, when he began his first term as vice president.

In 2000, Gore ran for president against Republican George W. Bush. In one of the closest races in U.S. history, Gore lost the election. Since then, he has worked primarily as an environmental activist. As a result of his efforts to address the problem of climate change, he was awarded the Nobel Peace Prize in 2007.

struggles under Bush's leadership. Most of Perot's supporters had the same complaints about Bush. If they were not voting for Perot, they would have likely supported Clinton instead. This meant that Perot's candidacy was taking potential votes away from Clinton. While Perot stood clearly in third place overall, his participation closed the gap somewhat between Clinton and Bush.

Nonetheless, Clinton ran a strong campaign in the weeks leading up to the November 3 election. In the three presidential debates held that October, he impressed audiences with his clearly stated plans to improve the country's economy and health care system.

George H. W. Bush (left) and Ross Perot (center) were unable to match Clinton's strong performance in the 1992 presidential debates.

On Election Day, Bill and Hillary watched closely as the results came in from each state. Eventually, the final count was in. Clinton won the election with 69 percent of the **electoral** vote. He had been chosen the 42nd president of the United States.

A Rocky Start

After his **inauguration** on January 20, 1993, Clinton began working on some of his plans for the country. One of his first efforts was an attempt to provide universal health insurance to all U.S. citizens. Such a program would ensure that everyone in the country could always

TODAY'S PERSPECTIVE

In the 1992 election, Bill Clinton and George H. W. Bush competed as rivals with vastly different political views. Years later, after both men had left office, they developed a friendship in spite of their many disagreements about government. In 2004, Clinton and Bush worked together to lead relief efforts after a powerful tsunami caused massive damage in southern Asia. While traveling through Asia, they spent time debating issues and sharing opinions. They came together again the following year to assist relief efforts after Hurricane Katrina hit the United States along the Gulf Coast. Since then, they have been good friends, exchanging letters frequently and greeting each other warmly at political events.

The Clinton health care plan was intended to provide medical care to all citizens who needed it.

afford the health care they needed. Hillary Clinton was one of the program's main creators. Unlike many first ladies who had come before her, she played a very active role in the government during her husband's administration. To the Clintons' disappointment, Congress rejected the proposed Health Security Act. This failure marked a difficult beginning to Clinton's first term in office.

President Clinton faced another challenge early in 1994. He was accused of participating in illegal business practices during his time as governor. At that time, he had invested in a housing development company called Whitewater. Rumors were now spreading that he had used his power as governor to illegally assist his business partners. U.S. attorney general Janet Reno soon approved an official investigation into the matter. A lawyer named Kenneth Starr was put in charge of the investigation, but it was eventually determined that there was not enough evidence against Clinton.

Despite early setbacks, President Clinton accomplished a great deal during his first four years in office. He proposed and supported many major **bills** that passed through Congress. The laws addressed many concerns, including crime prevention, environmental issues, and improvements to the education system. Clinton succeeded in raising the country's minimum wage and reducing the government's **deficit**.

Clinton also worked to improve relationships with other countries and spread peace throughout the

President Clinton worked hard to bring positive change to the country during his first term in office.

world. In 1993, he invited Israeli prime minister Yitzhak Rabin and Palestine Liberation Organization chairman Yasir Arafat to Washington, D.C. When Israel had been founded in 1948, it was formed in part from land that had belonged to Palestine. Since then, Palestinians and Israelis had been fighting over this land. At the 1993 meeting, Rabin and Arafat signed an agreement to give the Palestinians some control over the area. The agreement did not end the conflict permanently, but it helped calm some tensions in the region.

In 1995, Clinton sent representatives to Europe to begin peace talks between Bosnia, Croatia, and Serbia. These nations were in the middle of a violent struggle for control of land. Thanks in part to the U.S. involvement, the three nations signed a peace agreement on November 21, 1995.

Another Term

As a result of his many accomplishments, President Clinton remained very popular among Americans as the end of his first term neared. In 1996, he ran for reelection against Republican challenger Bob Dole and, once more, Ross Perot.

Clinton's past was again a major obstacle in the election. Though the Whitewater investigation had not turned up any proof that Clinton had broken the law, it still made some voters feel that the president might be secretive or untrustworthy. In addition, an Arkansas state employee named Paula Jones accused Clinton of having

During each presidential election, the leading candidates face off in a series of debates about the issues of the day. See page 60 for a link to watch video footage and read transcripts of the debates between Bill Clinton and Bob Dole during the 1996 campaign.

treated her unfairly after she turned down his romantic advances when he was governor. These continuing scandals damaged the president's reputation. However, most voters felt that his political accomplishments more than made up for his personal troubles. On November 5, he easily defeated Dole and Perot, winning more than 70 percent of the electoral vote.

President Clinton's successful first term gave him an advantage over his opponents in the 1996 election.

CHAPTER 4

MOVING ON

Chelsea Clinton stood by her
father's side as he was sworn in
for his second term as president.

As HE HEADED INTO HIS second term, everything seemed to be looking up for President Clinton. Thanks in part to his leadership, the economy was growing and crime statistics were dropping. The country was experiencing a very low unemployment rate, and polls showed that voters were mostly satisfied with the president's job performance. But Clinton's winning streak soon came to an end when he faced his biggest scandal yet.

White House intern Monica Lewinsky was at the center of the biggest scandal of President Clinton's career.

Impeached

In 1998, Kenneth Starr expanded his investigation into President Clinton's past. Starr began examining rumors that Clinton had been romantically involved with a young White House intern named Monica Lewinsky. Clinton repeatedly denied these accusations, even when he was testifying under **oath**. Lewinsky also denied the charges. However, Starr's investigation soon produced proof that both had been lying. In addition, it was revealed that the president had persuaded Lewinsky to lie.

Lying under oath is a serious crime. Pressuring someone else to lie under oath is considered obstruction of justice, which is also a crime. The House of Representatives voted on December 11–12, 1998, to impeach Clinton for these crimes. This meant that he would be put on trial before the Senate. If he was found guilty, he would be forced to leave office.

Clinton was only the second president in U.S. history to be impeached, after Andrew Johnson in 1868. Americans were shocked to see their leader being charged with such serious crimes. The scandal was a major news event, and it sparked discussion across the nation. Polls revealed that most people

SPOTLIGHT ON

Kenneth Starr

After graduating from Duke University Law School in 1973, Kenneth Starr began a long career as a government lawyer and judge. In 1994, he was chosen to lead the investigation into President Bill Clinton's business dealings with the Whitewater company. Though the president was not charged with any crimes as a result of this investigation, 11 other people were found guilty of various charges. Among them were some of Clinton's business partners.

Starr later expanded his investigation to include accusations of a romantic relationship between Clinton and White House intern Monica Lewinsky. As the scandal drew national attention, Starr soon became a household name. Many people accused him of leaking information about the investigation to the press and attempting to pursue his own Republican political goals by attacking the president. This criticism led him to resign from the case in 1999.

thought Clinton had broken the law and were disappointed in his behavior. However, most people still believed that he was doing a great job as president. The country's economy was strong and growing even stronger. Unemployment rates were lower than they had been in many years.

In February 1999, the Senate voted whether or not Clinton was guilty of the crimes for which he had been impeached. If two-thirds of the Senate voted him guilty, Clinton would be removed from office. However, less than half of the Senate voted against him, and he was **acquitted** on all charges. He apologized to the country for his wrongdoings, and his approval ratings remained extremely high for the rest of his time in office. Once again, he had avoided political disaster.

Around the nation, millions of Americans closely followed the events of President Clinton's impeachment trial.

Second Term Successes

Clinton's impeachment was not the only remarkable event of his second term. He continued to provide strong leadership for the country before and after his trial. During his final years in office, he focused heavily on foreign policy issues. In late 1998, he ordered bombings in Iraq, whose leaders were refusing to allow United Nations inspectors to search for dangerous weapons. The same year, Clinton helped negotiate peace between two rival political groups in Northern Ireland. In 2000, he became the first president to visit Vietnam since the end of the Vietnam War in 1975.

A VIEW FROM ABROAD

The neighboring countries of Ireland and the United Kingdom share a long and complicated history. Today, the northern portion of Ireland is a part of the United Kingdom, while the rest of the region exists as a separate nation. Some of Northern Ireland's people want to reunite with the rest of Ireland, while others are loyal to the United Kingdom. In the 1960s, these two groups began a major conflict that often escalated into violence during the following decades.

Throughout his presidency, Bill Clinton made it a priority to help end the conflict in Northern Ireland. He visited Ireland several times to meet with leaders from both groups and help them negotiate with one another. Clinton was well liked by people on both sides of the conflict, and his participation helped lead to a landmark peace agreement in 1998.

In the presidential election of 2000, Vice President Al Gore ran against George W. Bush, the son of former president George H. W. Bush. Bush won a close election and replaced Clinton as president in 2001. As Clinton concluded his presidency, he thought about what he would do next.

Forming a Foundation

After a long and successful political career, Clinton decided to turn his attention to **philanthropy**. He wanted to continue working on many of the same goals he'd had throughout his career in office. These included improvements to health care and education, eliminating poverty, and protecting the environment. So in 2001, he formed the William J. Clinton Foundation. Since then, the foundation has addressed a wide variety of global issues through a series of smaller programs called initiatives.

For example, the Clinton Health Access Initiative was formed to fight the spread of HIV/AIDS. It has since expanded to address other health issues, too. The Clinton Development Initiative helps farmers in poor countries purchase seeds, fertilizer, and other supplies. This increases the amount of food available to people in those regions. The Clinton Economic Opportunity Initiative encourages the growth of small businesses. The Clinton Global Initiative (CGI) brings together influential people from around the world to work to solve global problems. These and other initiatives of the Clinton Foundation have had a major impact on the world.

BILL CLINTON'S 2012 DEMOCRATIC NATIONAL CONVENTION SPEECH

The public reacted very warmly to Bill Clinton's speech at the 2012 Democratic National Convention. This illustrated the positive feelings that much of the country still had for the former president. The speech stands in contrast to Clinton's poor performance at the 1988 convention. It shows just how far he had come since then. See page 60 for a link to watch the entire speech online.

Clinton himself participates in many of the foundation's efforts. He regularly travels around the world to raise awareness and funding, and he meets with top leaders and thinkers to discuss important issues. Though he has been out of office for many years, Bill Clinton continues to have an impact on the world.

In 2010, Clinton visited Haiti to assist with relief efforts after a powerful earthquake devastated the country.

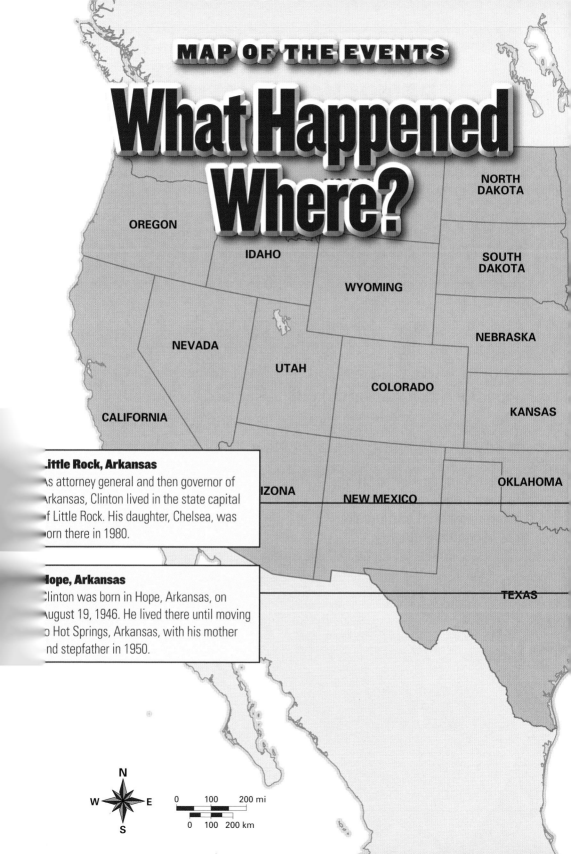

MAP OF THE EVENTS

What Happened Where?

NORTH DAKOTA

OREGON

IDAHO

SOUTH DAKOTA

WYOMING

NEVADA

NEBRASKA

UTAH

COLORADO

CALIFORNIA

KANSAS

Little Rock, Arkansas
As attorney general and then governor of Arkansas, Clinton lived in the state capital of Little Rock. His daughter, Chelsea, was born there in 1980.

IZONA

OKLAHOMA

NEW MEXICO

Hope, Arkansas
Clinton was born in Hope, Arkansas, on August 19, 1946. He lived there until moving to Hot Springs, Arkansas, with his mother and stepfather in 1950.

TEXAS

N
W   E
S

0   100   200 mi
0   100   200 km

Washington, D.C.
Clinton first visited the U.S. capital in 1963 as a participant in Boys State. He later returned as U.S. president after winning the election in 1992.

VERMONT

MAINE

NESOTA

NH

WISCONSIN

MA

MICHIGAN

NEW YORK
New Haven

RI

CT

IOWA

PENNSYLVANIA

NEW JERSEY

OHIO

INDIANA

DELAWARE

ILLINOIS

Washington, D.C. ✪

MARYLAND

WEST
VIRGINIA

MISSOURI

VIRGINIA

KENTUCKY

NORTH
CAROLINA

TENNESSEE

ARKANSAS

SOUTH
CAROLINA

Little Rock

Hope

MISSISSIPPI

GEORGIA

New Haven, Connecticut
Yale Law School is located in New Haven, Connecticut. Bill Clinton met his wife, Hillary, while they were students there.

ALABAMA

LOUISIANA

FLORIDA

A Lasting Legacy

Bill Clinton's presidency marked one of the most economically successful periods in recent U.S. history.

Though Bill Clinton dealt with several scandals while in office, his presidency was largely successful. Many people in the country look back fondly on his

THE CLINTON FOUNDATION HAS HELPED

accomplishments. While Clinton was in office, the nation experienced a period of peace and prosperity. His leadership brought about low unemployment rates, low **inflation**, and low crime rates. Fewer people needed welfare assistance, and more people than ever were able to purchase their own homes. Clinton also helped balance the government's budget for the first time in many years. This meant that the government was bringing in more money than it was spending. Such a situation had not occurred since 1970.

Clinton's work has not ended. In 2013, the Clinton Foundation expanded to include Hillary and Chelsea as major forces within the organization. Working with his wife and daughter, Bill's efforts continue to affect the United States and the world.

Former president Clinton meets face to face with people all around the world on behalf of the Clinton Foundation.

PEOPLE IN MORE THAN 180 NATIONS.

INFLUENTIAL INDIVIDUALS

Virginia Cassidy

Virginia Cassidy (1923–1994) was the mother of President Bill Clinton. After her husband was killed in a car accident during her pregnancy with Bill, she went back to school in order to get a better job to support her son.

George H. W. Bush (1924–) was the 41st president of the United States. Though he and Bill Clinton were bitter rivals during the 1992 election, they later developed a close friendship.

Kenneth Starr (1946–) was the lawyer who investigated Bill Clinton during the Whitewater and Monica Lewinsky scandals. He was criticized for using the cases to support his own political goals.

Hillary Rodham Clinton (1947–) is the wife of Bill Clinton. After her husband's presidency, she began a highly successful political career of her own, serving in Congress and as the U.S. secretary of state.

Al Gore Jr. (1948–) was vice president of the United States under Bill Clinton. At the end of Clinton's second term, Gore ran for president but was defeated by George W. Bush. He then left politics to devote himself to environmental activism.

Hillary Rodham Clinton

Al Gore Jr.

1946

William Jefferson Blythe III is born in Hope, Arkansas.

1963

Bill Clinton meets President John F. Kennedy while visiting Washington, D.C., as part of the Boys State program.

1975

Bill Clinton and Hillary Rodham are married at their home in Fayetteville, Arkansas.

1976

Clinton campaigns for and wins the position of Arkansas attorney general.

1978

Clinton is elected governor of Arkansas.

1996

Clinton is reelected president.

1998

Clinton is impeached on charges of lying under oath and obstruction of justice.

1999

The Senate acquits Clinton on all charges.

1968

Clinton graduates from Georgetown University.

1970

Clinton starts law school at Yale University, where he begins dating a fellow student named Hillary Rodham.

1974

Clinton runs for a seat in the U.S. House of Representatives but loses the election.

1980

Clinton fails to win reelection as Arkansas governor; Chelsea Clinton is born.

1982

Clinton successfully runs for governor of Arkansas.

1992

Clinton defeats George H. W. Bush and Ross Perot in the presidential election.

2001

Clinton leaves office after his second term and establishes the William J. Clinton Foundation to support his philanthropic causes.

2012

Clinton delivers a celebrated speech in support of President Barack Obama at the 2012 Democratic National Convention.

LIVING HISTORY

Primary sources provide firsthand evidence about a topic. Witnesses to a historical event create primary sources. They include autobiographies, newspaper reports of the time, oral histories, photographs, and memoirs. A secondary source analyzes primary sources, and is one step or more removed from the event. Secondary sources include textbooks, encyclopedias, and commentaries. To view the following primary and secondary sources, go to www.factsfornow.scholastic.com. Enter the keywords **Bill Clinton** and look for the Living History logo ∑.

∑ Bill Clinton's 1988 Democratic National Convention Speech
Bill Clinton was a rising political star when he was chosen to deliver the nomination speech at the 1988 Democratic National Convention. His long speech lacked focus and bored the audience. As a result, it was widely mocked in the following days.

∑ Bill Clinton's 2012 Democratic National Convention Speech
Twenty-four years after his widely disliked speech at the 1988 Democratic National Convention, Bill Clinton returned to the same stage to deliver a much more successful nominating speech for President Barack Obama.

∑ Martin Luther King Jr.'s "I Have a Dream" Speech
Martin Luther King Jr.'s August 28, 1963, speech from the Lincoln Memorial in Washington, D.C., stands as one of the most powerful speeches of all time. As a young man, Bill Clinton was so moved by King's words that he memorized the entire speech.

∑ The 1996 Presidential Debates
In 1996, Bill Clinton ran for reelection against Republican challenger Bob Dole. Clinton's strong performance in the presidential debates helped him win the election.

RESOURCES

Books

Doak, Robin S. *Hillary Clinton*. New York: Children's Press, 2013.

Dunn, Joeming W. *Bill Clinton: 42nd U.S. President*. Edina, MN: Magic Wagon, 2012.

Venezia, Mike. *Bill Clinton: Forty-Second President, 1993–2001*. New York: Children's Press, 2008.

Visit this Scholastic Web site for more information on Bill Clinton:
www.factsfornow.scholastic.com
Enter the keywords Bill Clinton

GLOSSARY

acquitted (uh-KWIT-id) found not guilty of a crime

bills (BILZ) written plans for new laws

deficit (DEF-i-sit) a situation where more money has been spent than comes in

drafted (DRAFT-id) made to join the armed forces

economy (i-KAHN-uh-mee) the system of buying, selling, making things, and managing money in a place

electoral (uh-lek-TOR-uhl) related to the electoral college, the body that officially elects the president and vice president according to the public's vote

inauguration (in-aw-gyuh-RAY-shuhn) a formal ceremony in which a government official is sworn into office

incumbent (in-KUHM-buhnt) the current holder of an office

inflation (in-FLAY-shuhn) a general increase in prices, causing money to be worth less

oath (OHTH) a solemn, formal promise or declaration

philanthropy (fuh-LAN-thruh-pee) the act of helping others by giving time or money to causes and charities

polls (POHLZ) surveys of people's opinions or beliefs

primary (PRYE-mair-ee) an election to choose a party candidate who will run in the general election

recession (ri-SESH-uhn) a time when business slows down and more workers than usual are unemployed

Page numbers in *italics* indicate illustrations.

ABOUT THE AUTHOR

Josh Gregory writes and edits books for kids. He lives in Chicago, Illinois.